3D PAPER CRAFT PATRICK PASQUES

Animals of Africa

Animali d'Africa

Make your own paper animals / *Crea da solo i tuoi animali*

promopress

3D Paper Craft
ANIMALS OF AFRICA
ANIMALI D'AFRICA

Promopress is a commercial brand of:
Promotora de prensa internacional S.A.
C/Ausiàs March 124
08013 Barcelona (Spain)
T: (+34) 93 245 14 64
F: (+34) 93 265 48 93
info@promopress.es
www.promopresseditions.com

Copyright © 2013 by Un Dimanche Après Midi -
Editions Tutti Frutti.
Copyright © 2013 English & Italian
editions by Promopress.

Editorial project by Editions Tutti Frutti
Chief editor: Alexis Faja
Executive editor: Lorraine Desgardin
Author: Patrick Pasques

Design & layout: Satèl·lit bcn -
Laura Klamburg & Meri Iannuzzi

ISBN 978-84-92810-75-8
Printed in China

> CONTENTS > SOMMARIO

> PRACTICAL TIPS > CONSIGLI PRATICI

> This book features 10 colour templates and 10 black and white templates to colour in.
> In questo quaderno ci sono 10 sagome colorate e 10 sagome in bianco e nero da colorare.

> Materials needed > Materiale

> Pair of scissors
> Un paio di forbici

Liquid glue
Colla liquida

Cyanolit superglue®
Colla cyanolit®

Glue stick
Colla stick

Felt-tip pens
Pennarelli

> What to do > Come fare

A
> Cut out the template along the outer lines.
  Cut the edge of the flaps marked with red.
> Ritaglia seguendo i bordi esterni della sagoma.
  Taglia i bordi delle linguette con un tratto rosso.

B
> Fold all of the flaps upwards.
> Piega tutte le linguette all'indietro.

C
> Put the model together and glue the flaps into place.
> Metti il modello in forma e incolla le linguette.

D
> Assemble the different parts of the model.
> Metti insieme i diversi pezzi della sagoma.

> Recommendations > Raccomandazioni

> Cut slowly and near the lines. Don't use too much glue. Every time you apply the glue, wait a few seconds for it to dry. Dry your hands using a clean cloth. Take your time to build the model properly.
> Ritaglia piano, attorno ai bordi. Non usare troppa colla. Attendi qualche secondo tra un'incollatura e l'altra. Usa un panno pulito per asciugarti le dita. Prenditi il tempo necessario per completare un bel montaggio.

Buffalo Bufalo

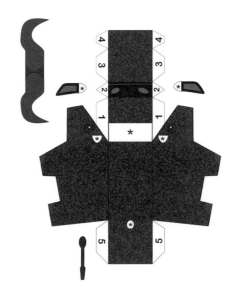

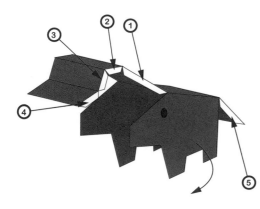

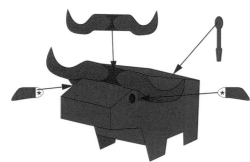

Dromedary Dromedario

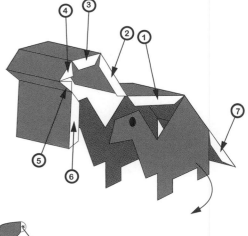

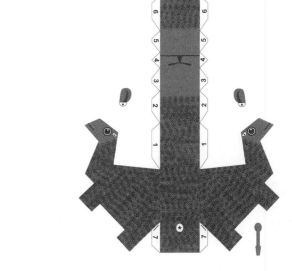

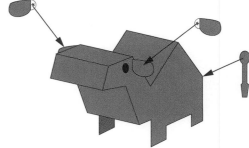

1

2

3

Elephant Elefante

Giraffe Giraffa

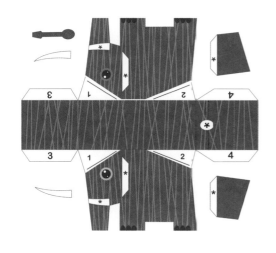

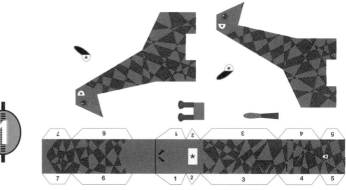

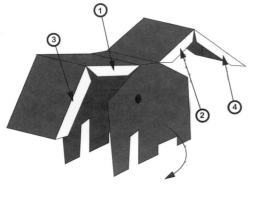

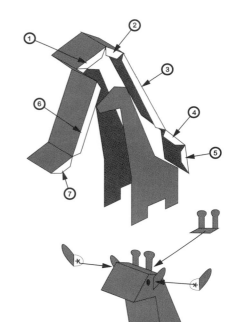

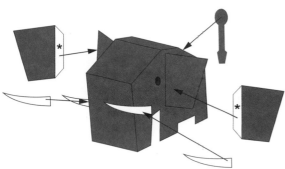

Hippopotamus Ippopotamo

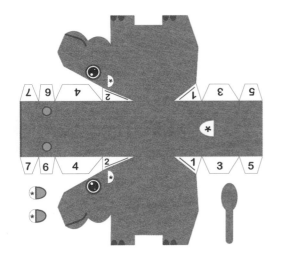

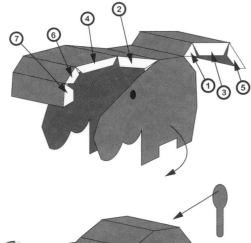

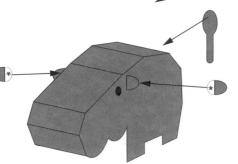

Leopard Leopardo

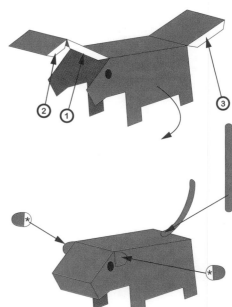

Lion Leone

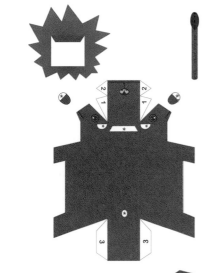

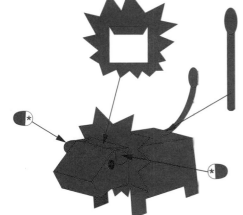

Warthog Facocero

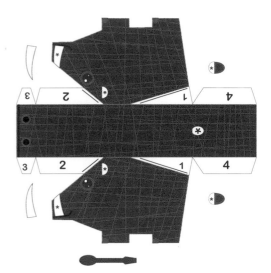

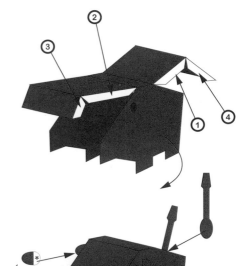

Rhinoceros Rinoceronte

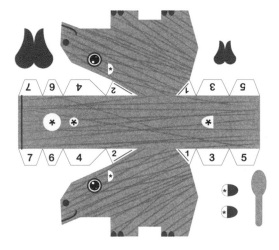

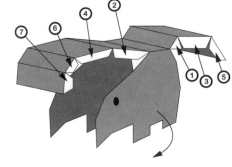

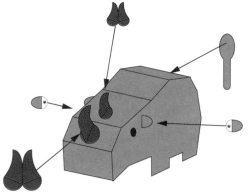

Zebra

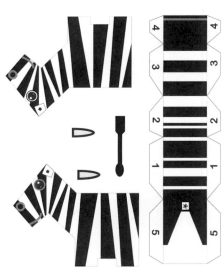

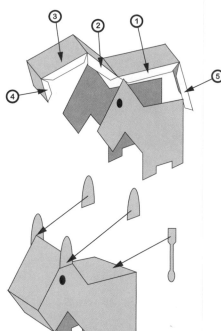

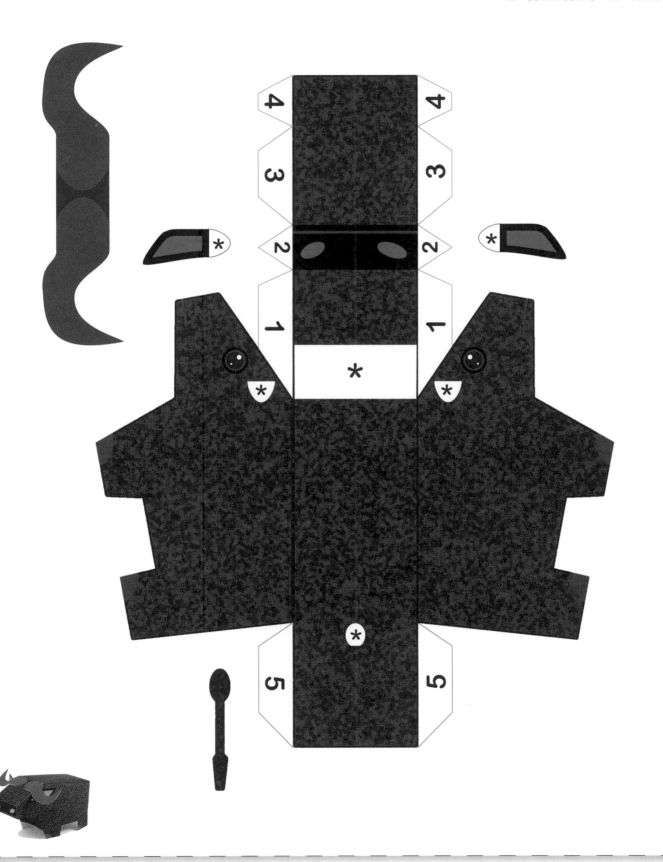

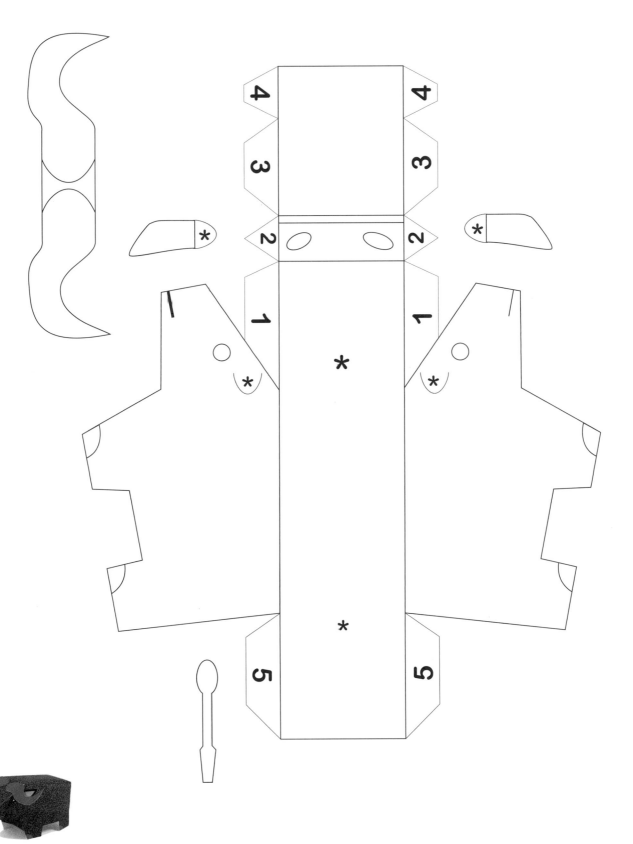

Dromedary Dromedario

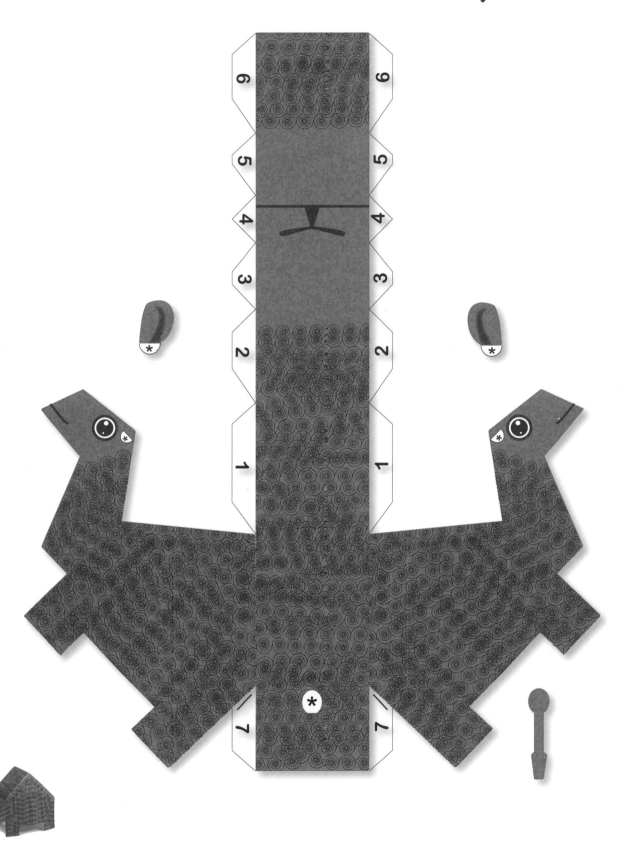

Dromedary Dromedario

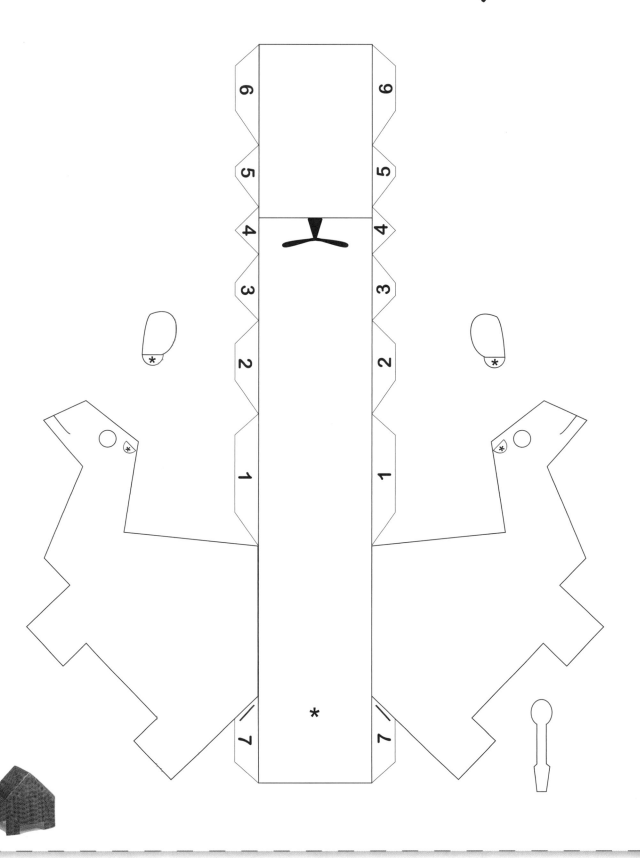

Elephant Elefante

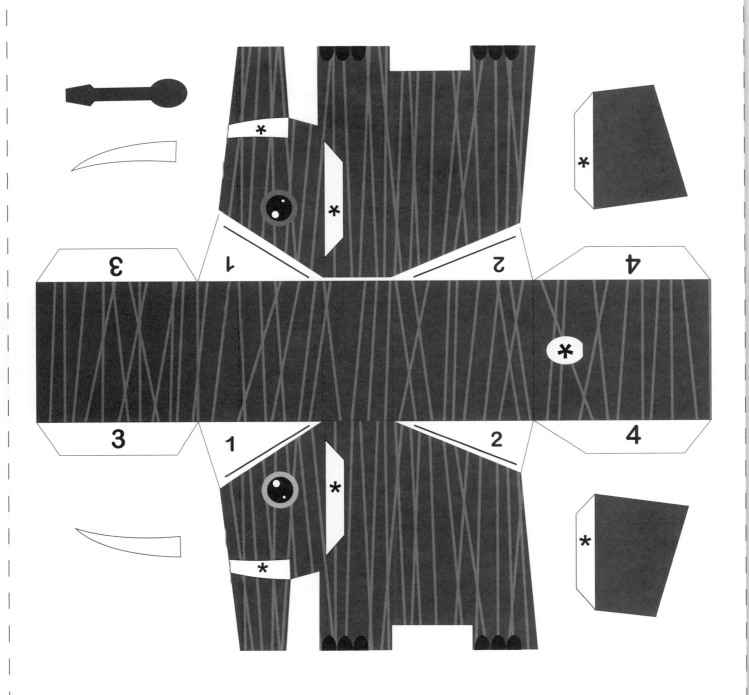

Elephant Elefante

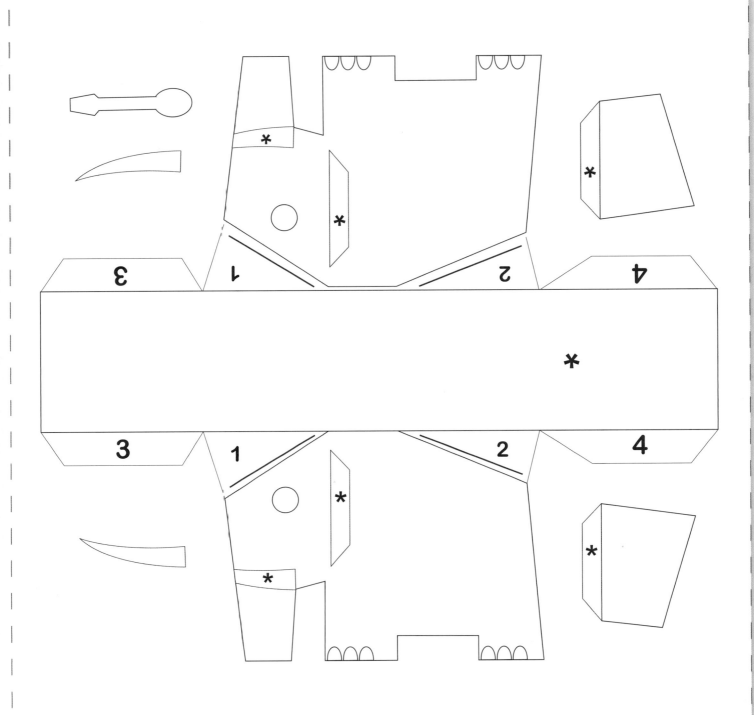

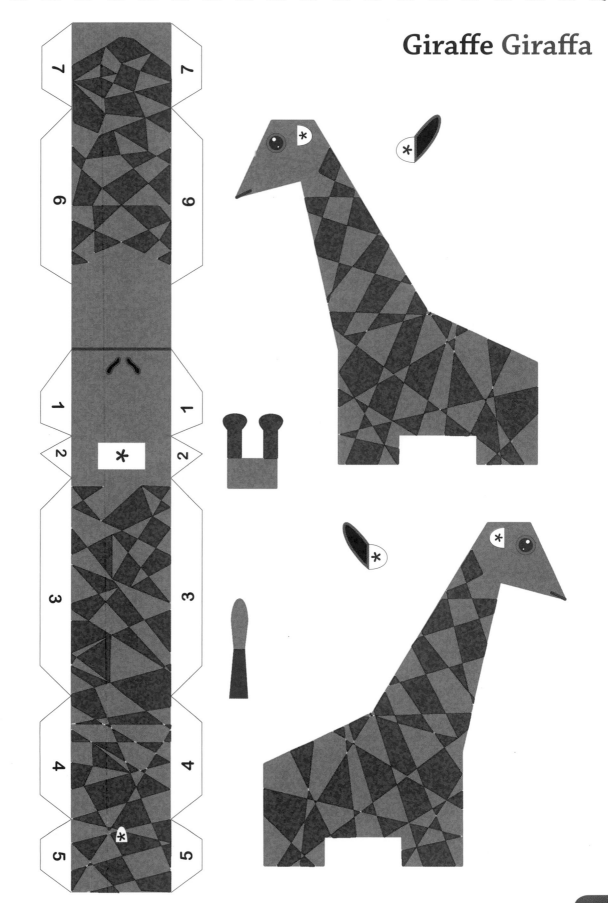

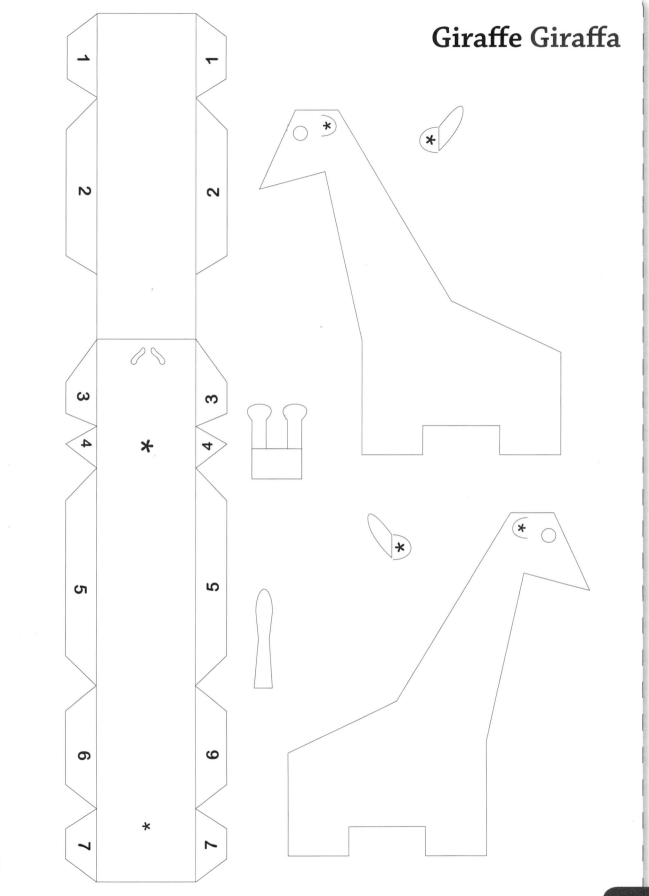

Giraffe Giraffa

Hippopotamus Ippopotamo

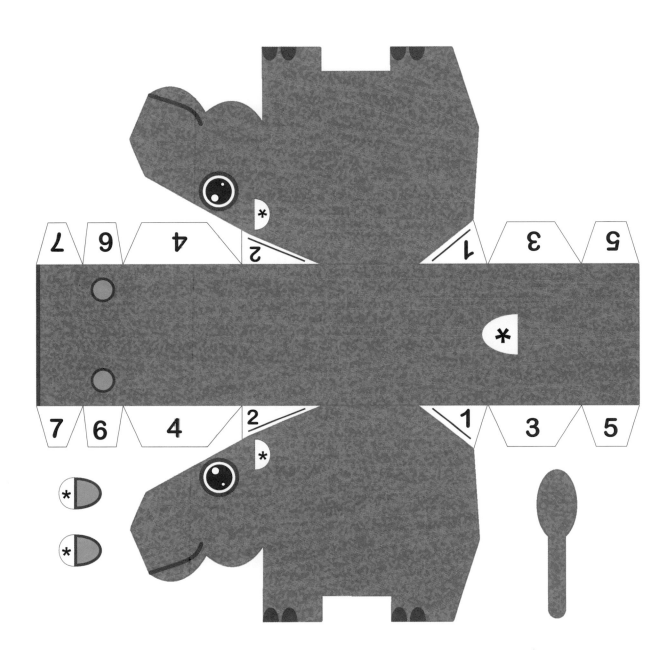

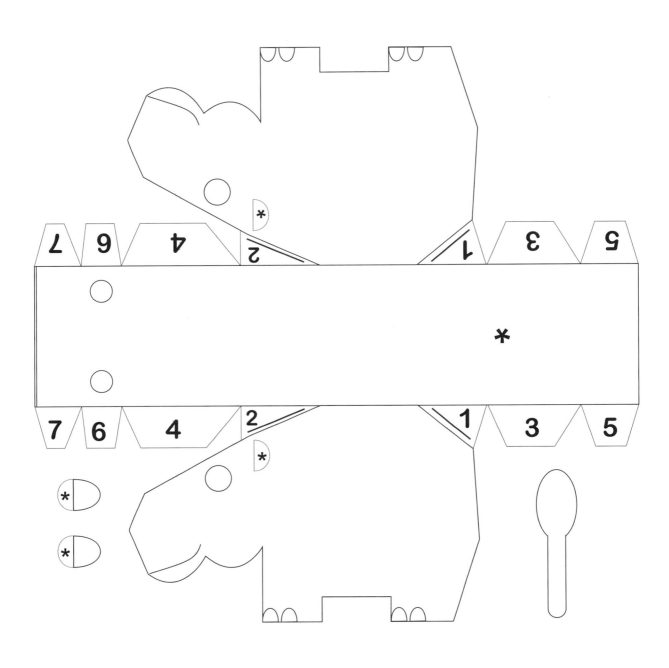

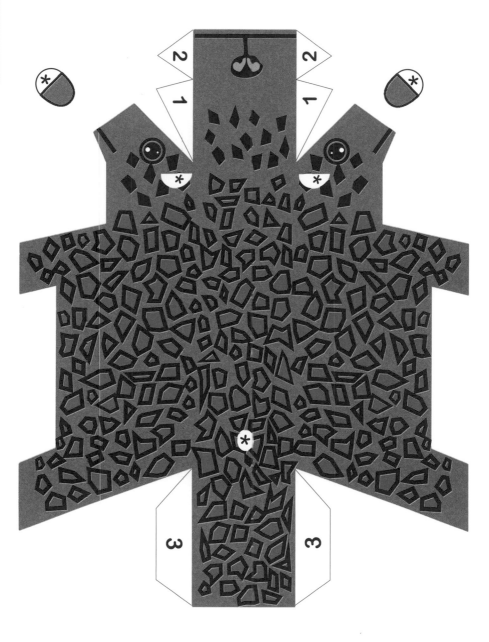

2

2

1

1

*

*

*

*

*

3

3

31

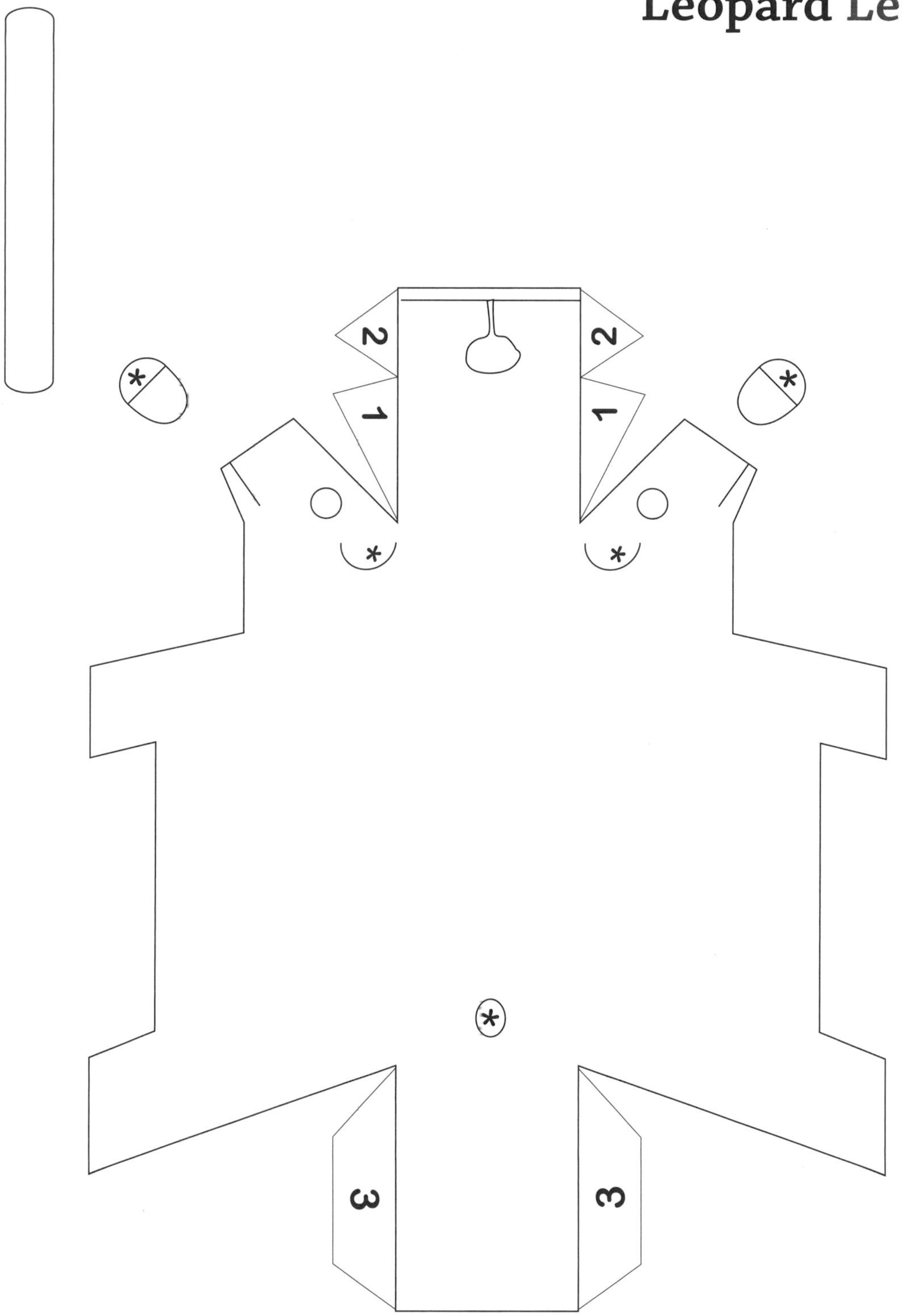

Lion Leone

2 1 2 1

3 3

33

Lion Leone

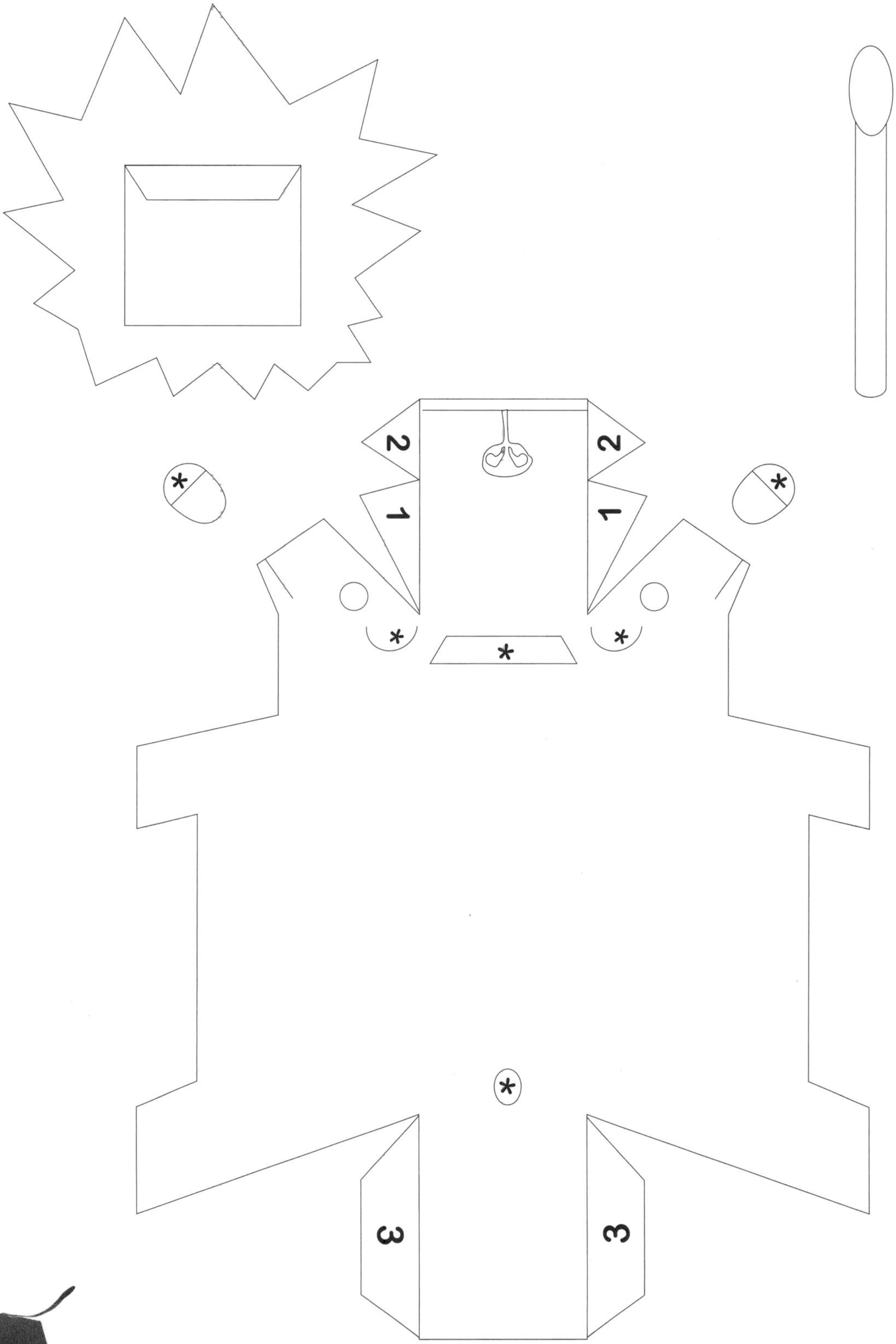

2

1

2

1

*

*

*

*

*

*

3

3

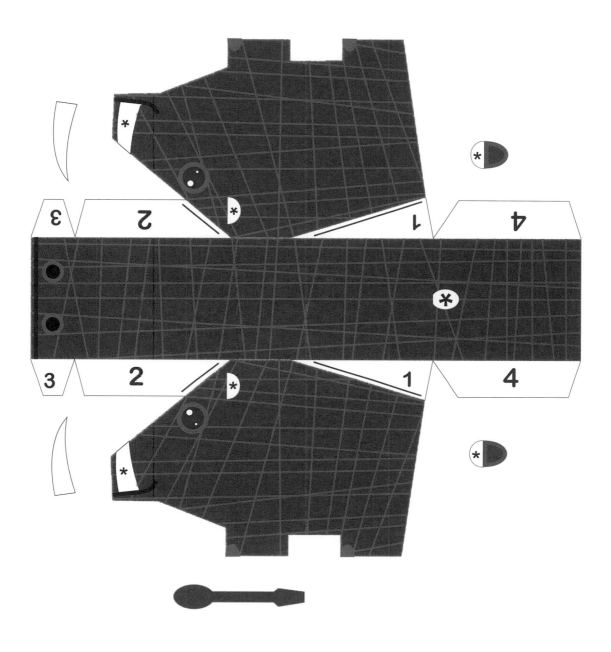

Warthog Facocero

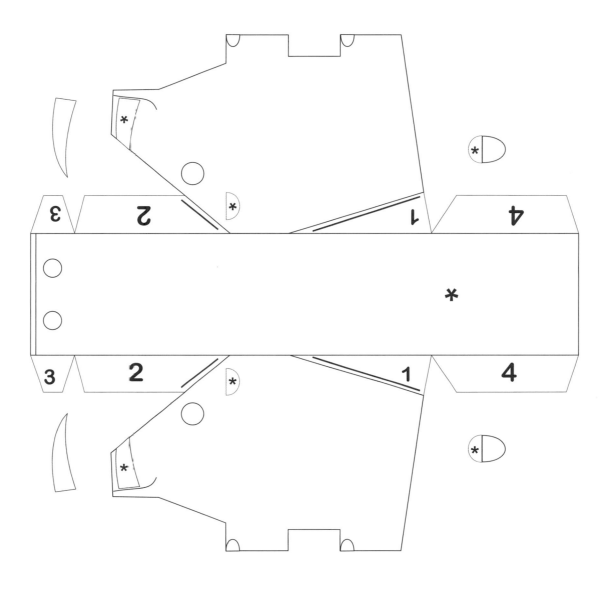

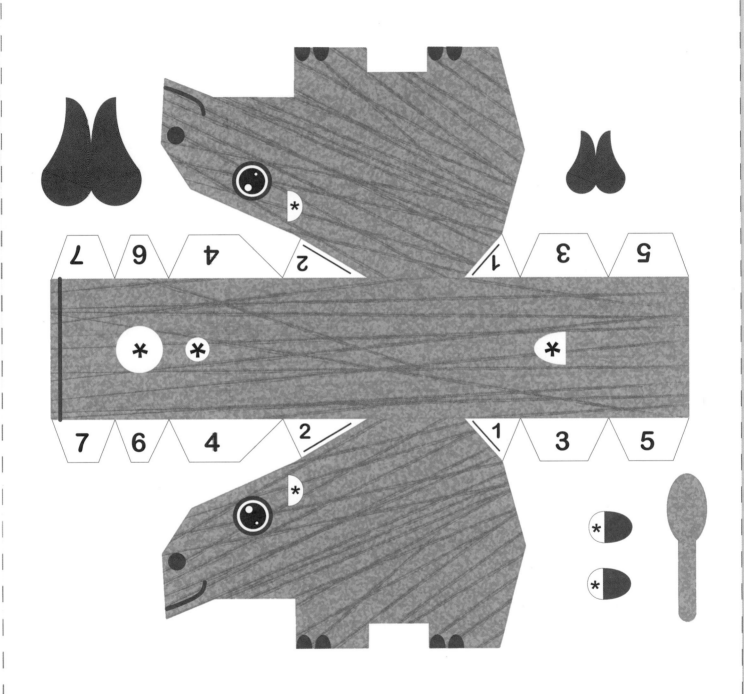

Rhinoceros Rinoceronte

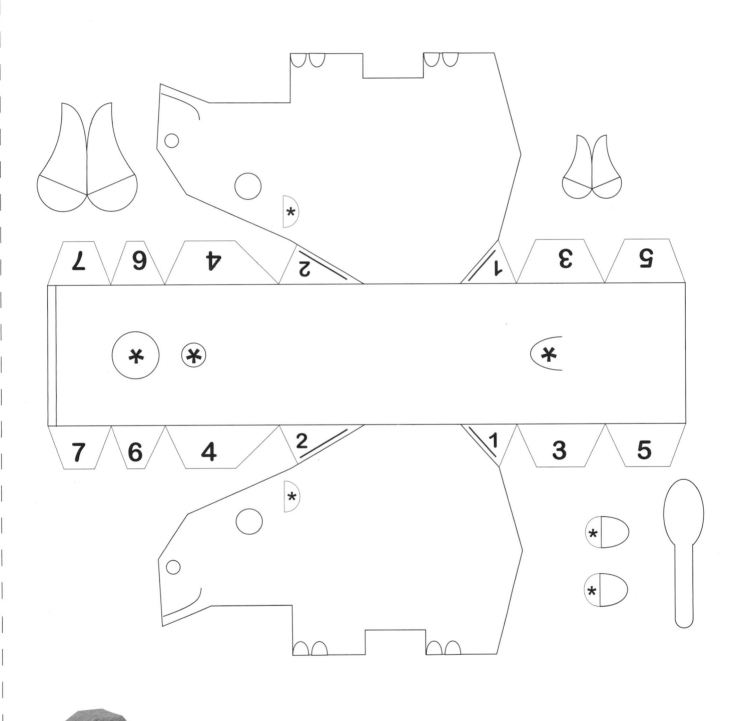

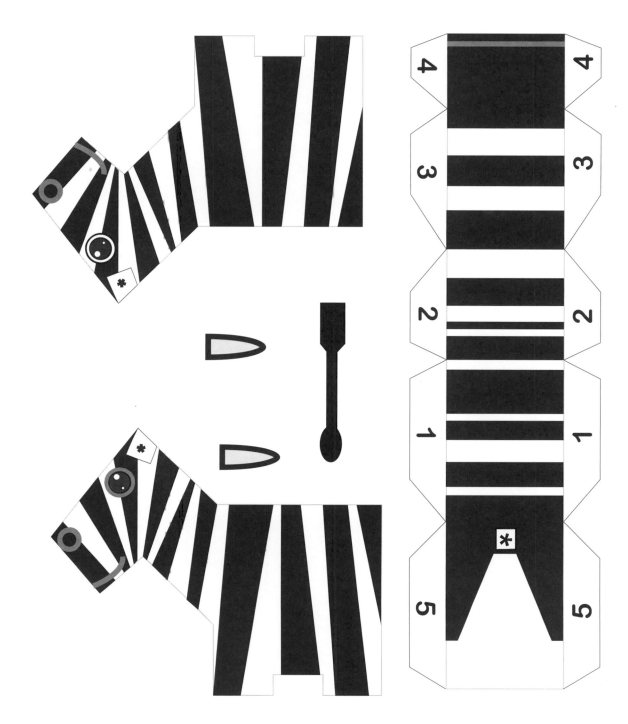

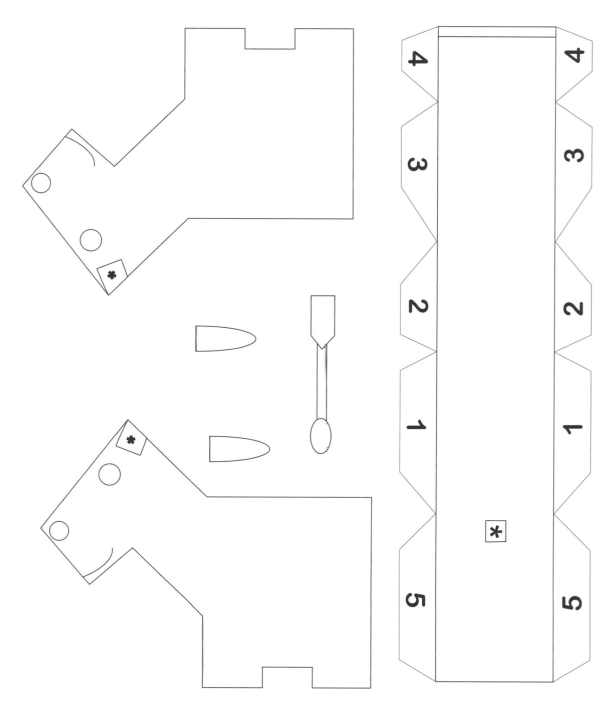